THE MINISTRY IN *You*

BRINGING OUT WHAT GOD PLACED WITHIN

LYLE DUKES

HWP.
Harvest Word Publishing

Woodbridge, Virginia

Published in Woodbridge, Virginia by Harvest Word Publishing.

ISBN: 1-888918-12-8

Printed in the United States of America

THE MINISTRY IN You

CONTENTS

ACKNOWLEDGEMENTS

I would like to thank all of the powerful ministries of integrity and the mentors that I have had in my life. You have proven, by example, what it means to live out the ministry in you. I want to thank my wife Deborah, Co-Pastor of our church—I love you, sweetheart. To my "PK" Brittany, thank you for the willful sacrifice of your Daddy-Pastor over the years.

To my mom and dad, Edwin Dukes and Priscilla Lutz, you have added much to my life. I love you both. To my beautiful sisters, whom I was born between, Angel and Faith, you have helped shape my life more than you know. To Bishop Carver and Co-Pastor Lorene Poindexter, you are my spiritual parents, not to mention the best in-laws anyone could have—I love you. A shout out to Robin, my sister-in-law, you keep me laughing.

To the Harvest Life Changers Church and the Lyle and Deborah Dukes Ministries Partners, thank you for your prayers and support. To my editorial team—Lori Brooks, Nichelle Gardner, Christine Mallory, Shenell Shepard and Jim Gillis—thanks once again. To Tamara Jones, many thanks for your technical assistance.

Lyle Dukes
Woodbridge, Virginia

INTRODUCTION

Over the last several years there has been a remarkable deluge of dialogue concerning purpose. It seems to have struck a cord of the central nervous system of mankind. Several didactic and edifying works have been authored, focus groups have been formed and instructive systematic programs have been offered and implemented, and they are all about purpose.

I celebrate the discovery of purpose as much as anyone, but it should be understood that you may possess a purpose—and even be conversant of what that purpose is—and not live it out through your life. Do not get me wrong; I believe that God has issued a definite purpose for everyone. I do not believe, however, that everyone is fulfilling his or her God-given purpose. The fulfillment of purpose is what this book is about.

Ministry is the fulfillment of purpose. Moses was considered the great deliverer of Israel and his purpose was reflected through his leadership ministry. John the Baptist's purpose was made manifest through his ministry of baptizing and preaching about the soon coming King. Paul was the great Apostle to the Gentiles. His purpose came through in his letters, travels and nurturing

ministry. Even our Lord Jesus Christ, the savior of mankind—
emerged through his ministry of 3 1/2 years climaxing in his
death, burial and resurrection. Ministry brings purpose alive.
In fact, the power of purpose is only evident through ministry.
Your "calling" or purpose has a mandate to be satisfied.

"Wherefore the rather, brethren, give diligence to make your
calling and election sure..." 2 Peter 1:10

There is a ministry in you just waiting to come forth, a purpose
in you just waiting to be fulfilled. I honestly believe that each
individual is designed by God with the potential for purposeful
ministry. God has installed talents, gifts, abilities, drive,
temperament, initiative, discernment, levels of understanding,
capacity for multi-tasking, a threshold of pain, degrees of relational
adaptivity and even spiritual revelation in every human being.

All of these things (with others) will uniquely speak to
purpose and be used as instruments in ministry. These tools
will be employed to render service for the Kingdom. Now, there
is a process that must be deployed that will take the individual
through purpose discovery into the actual release of ministry.
The process deals with getting the vessel (or individual) in the
right posture to allow ministry to be produced through them.

"Who shall ascend into the hill of the Lord? or who shall stand in
his holy place? He that hath clean hands, and a pure heart; who
hath not lifted up his soul unto vanity, nor sworn deceitfully. He
shall receive the blessing from the Lord, and righteousness from

the God of his salvation." Psalm 24:3-5

This particular scripture gives us insight on how God views our service toward him. This Psalm of David makes reference to the "priestly" work of the Kingdom. If one were to minister in the temple (the Hill of the Lord) or even stand in the Holy Place, which is the job of the High Priest, there were spiritual requirements that had to be in place. Notice what God requires of those that he chose to minister through—clean hands and a pure heart. He did not mention education, church affiliation or even experience. These kinds of things may be important in the total scheme of things. However, God makes it clear that to minister for him, there must be, first and foremost, a strong spiritual foundation. Let's look at it.

CLEAN HANDS

The requirement of clean hands had to do with what we should do "outwardly" to be aligned with God's purpose and plan for our lives. It is necessary that we discipline ourselves to the point that the things that we can control about our lives are undeniably and indisputably brought under the auspices of righteousness. Naturally, hands are bodily components that we as human beings are responsible for. The level of "clean" had to do with extreme care since hands—because of their multifunction—are apt to become soiled and unhygienic.

When I was a child, my sister and I were made to go to the bathroom and wash our hands before sitting down at the table before dinner. When we came out of the bathroom we had to present our hands for inspection. Frequently, I was sent back to the bathroom because my hands were not clean. After repeating this process time and again, I finally came to the conclusion that "washed" hands may not be necessarily clean hands. The level of clean is established through careful washing. God expects us and even empowers us to uphold his standards so that we can maintain a posture where ministry can flow through us. This is something for which we are responsible.

> *"Prove all things; hold fast that which is good. Abstain from all appearance of evil."* 1 Thessalonians 5:21-22

A PURE HEART

The requirement of a pure heart has to deal with something that can only be done inwardly through our relationship with God. If we are ever to do ministry for God, then our hearts must be in sync with God's heart. The scriptures present God's view on his ministry tool, King David:

> *"And when he had removed him (King Saul), he raised up unto them David to be their king; to whom also he gave testimony, and said, I have found David the Son of Jesse, a man after mine own heart, which shall fulfil all my will."* Acts 13:22

God is looking for people that are sincere about him. He is searching for people that love him and just want to do his will. The Lord wants pure hearts, not perfect people. David, by no means was perfect, but he had a heart for God! This heart mandate is established through responding willfully to the Father while in a consistent walk with him. When a pure heart is present, ministry can emanate and purpose can manifest itself through the life of its proprietor.

CHAPTER ONE

LIVING UP IN A FALLEN WORLD

"Stand fast therefore in the liberty wherewith Christ hath made us free, and be not entangled again with the yoke of bondage."
Galatians 5:1

In our discussion of ministry, it must be observed that reaching the actual place of ministry is not achieved without difficulty. This is primarily because the tide and flow of the world, in which we live, is moving in the opposite direction. Therefore, just to live right is a struggle. Jesus states in St. Luke 21:17:

"And ye shall be hated of all men for my name's sake."

Now, when we dialogue concerning the performance of ministry, we are talking about a whole new level. The execution of the workings of ministry will emphatically face tremendous opposition! For ministry to be carried out effectively, it must reside in an individual that seeks to maintain a high level of righteousness. God will not anoint and release the gifts of ministry through anyone that is not striving, in a radical sense, to live according to God's holy ordinances. I have heard people say, "God can use anyone." That's true. He can use anyone, but He won't.

Check out the men and women that God has used throughout the Bible and through the chronology of time. They were individuals who were sincere and consecrated before the Lord. They were not perfect, but they were folks that could be considered as "extremist" by the world's standards.

Abraham, who left all his kindred on a word that God spoke to him, is a good example. Moses, who stayed in the mountain alone to talk to God for extended periods of time could be categorized as extreme. There was King David who wrote poems to God and was found dancing in the streets before the Lord among the common people.

Then there was John the Baptist, wearing camel's hair garments and eating locusts and wild honey. He baptized everyone who was willing in the Jordan River, declaring that "the Kingdom of God is at hand." The highly intelligent Apostle Paul followed a group of uneducated fisherman into a very new and questionable religious movement. This list goes on into our present time. Those who God uses in ministry, in most circles, are considered as zealous fanatics. However, this "upness" is required because we are in a fallen world.

A FALLEN WORLD

We all know that this is not the way it should have been. When Adam and Eve were in the Garden of Eden, the ministry that God gave flowed effortlessly out of them. Their lives were uniquely connected to ministering for and to God.

"And the Lord God took the man, and put him into the garden of Eden to dress it and to keep it." Genesis 2:15

"And out of the ground the Lord God formed every beast of the field, and every fowl of the air; and brought them unto Adam to see what he would call them: and whatsoever Adam called every living creature, that was the name thereof." Genesis 2:19

Adam and Eve's service unto God actually fit the environment in which they lived. There was no resistance—no going against the grain in that world. Things changed after Adam sinned.

The disobedience of Adam led to a fallen state for both the world and mankind. We became "jacked up" people living in a "jacked up" world. Suddenly, ministry for and to God did not match the world where we used to live. What was effortless and commonplace became a struggle and required a great effort of labor to bring to pass. Sacrifices and blood atonement were needed just to get mankind in a state of righteousness so that we could be used for God's service. Because of the perpetually descending and decaying state of the world and mankind, it appeared that ministry for God was placed on a high shelf in the cupboard of

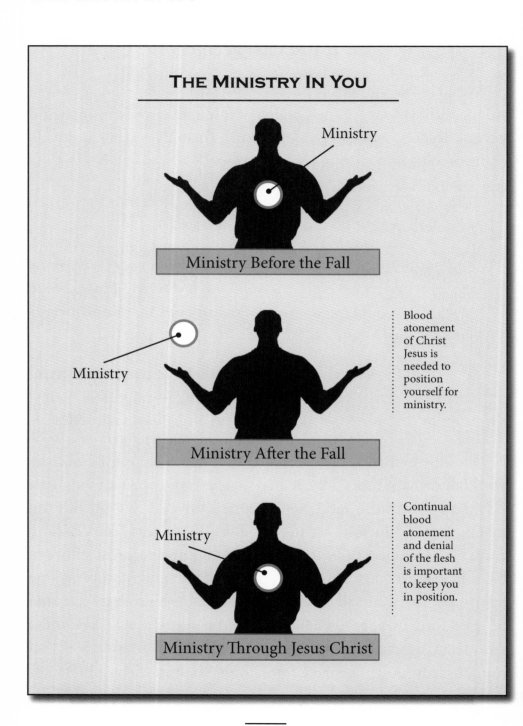

life. A strong effort, along with the grace and mercy of God, would be required to allow ministry to be released in us.

To reach this high level of service is one thing, but to maintain its standards is yet another thing. We must continue to shake off the fallen state because the gravity of a sinful world is all around us. The Lord Jesus tells the church at Ephesus in Revelation 2:2-5:

> *"I know thy works, and thy labor, and thy patience, and how thou canst not bear them which are evil...Nevertheless I have somewhat against thee, because thou hast left thy first love. Remember therefore from whence thou art fallen, and repent, and do the first works; or else I will come unto thee quickly, and will remove thy candlestick out of his place, except thou repent."*

So, ministry is for those that are willing to go the distance. Ministry requires a sacrifice. There is a ministry in you, but are you willing to go through the resistance of your flesh and the world to get to it and maintain it? Are you willing to work the talents that God gave you to bring this anointed level of service to pass? You can do it because Jesus Christ has made a way for you.

> *"Christ hath redeemed us from the curse of the law, being made a curse for us: for it is written, Cursed is every one that hangeth on a tree: That the blessing of Abraham might come on the Gentiles through Jesus Christ; that we might receive the promise of the Spirit through faith."* Galatians 3:13-14

Please understand that there is a powerful ministry inside of you. But it is going to take some effort to get it out. You must push yourself into a posture so that your calling will come to pass throughout the balance of your life.

"Who hath saved us, and called us with an holy calling, not according to our works, but according to his own purpose and grace, which was given us in Christ Jesus before the world began," 2 Timothy 1:9

"Wherefore the rather, brethren, give diligence to make your calling and election sure: for if ye do these things, ye shall never fall:" 2 Peter 1:10

"Create in me a clean heart, O God; and renew a right spirit within me." Psalm 51:10

CHAPTER TWO

MINISTRY:
YOUR REAL PURPOSE FOR LIVING

"Be not thou therefore ashamed of the testimony of our Lord, nor of me his prisoner: but be thou partaker of the afflictions of the gospel according to the power of God; Who hath saved us, and called us with an holy calling, not according to our works, but according to his own purpose and grace, which was given us in Christ Jesus before the world began," 2 Timothy 1:8-9

Ministry is a symphonic expression of the leading of the Holy Spirit that is carefully choreographed to optimize the gifted potential that God has placed within us. In other words, ministry is God working in us and it is evident that his work should be performed through us because there are so many gifts, talents and abilities in each living person. If this is the case, then everyone has a ministry. It is also clear that ministry is not limited to the confines of your local church building; wherever you are, God wants ministry to flow through you!

MINISTRY LEADS TO PURPOSE FULFILLMENT

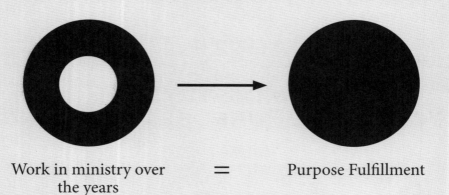

Work in ministry over   =   Purpose Fulfillment
        the years

INDIVIDUAL'S FULFILLMENT OF PURPOSE SYLLOGISM

Premise #1:   Individual possesses ministry

Premise #2:   Ministry is God working through individual

Premise #3:   It takes God to fulfill purpose

Conclusion: Individual's ministry fulfills purpose

The congregational preaching ministry, teaching ministry, administrative ministry and usher ministry are vital and very essential services designated for the local church. However, ministry goes beyond these borders because it is in you. Unless God has purposed for you to inhabit the four walls of the church twenty-four hours a day, seven days a week, you won't be fulfilling all that God has designed for your life through ministry.

"Ye are of God, little children, and have overcome them: because greater is he that is in you, than he that is in the world." 1 John 4:4

God doesn't just want to be great in you down at the local church. He wants to be great in you everywhere. We have allowed institutional teaching and preconceived ideas to conceptualize and limit our view of ministry. But ministry is whenever God works through you.

So, it is apparent that there are other ministries in which we take part. Here are a few examples: the husband ministry, the wife ministry, parent ministry, helping your cousin out of trouble ministry, being nice down at the supermarket ministry, praying for your co-workers to be saved ministry, paying your bills on time ministry, taking the burden off of your pastor ministry, loving your neighbor ministry and the list continues. When God uses you to be ministered through, that situation becomes the next ministry of which you are a part.

When you really get it, you will see that your purpose in life will be manifested through your pervasive and continuing ministry. All of the various external challenges of people problems and issues in life are uniquely connected to your purpose. For each challenge there is an internal solution that is found in the alcoves of ministry.

Many believe that they must go to a foreign country or obtain a certain position before they can start their ministry. I beg to differ. Ministry is very real right here and right now! It is your real purpose for living. I'm not saying that you can start calling yourself an ordained minister or a licensed preacher. I am, however, suggesting that the ministry of service and sermons of life start long before ordination. In fact, the real reason why a person is given a title is because they have already been proven. A title is just a label.

When I was growing up in the country, I can remember many of my relatives "canning" strawberry preserves. They would pack glass jars with strawberries, sugar and other ingredients. After this, they would vacuum seal the jar. To get the top off later would almost give you a hernia (smile). They would label each jar with the word, "strawberry." It is interesting that the label only described what was already in the jar! A title does not transform the product. It just simply labels it. A preacher or a ministry should radiate that level of service long before the actual office or title is bestowed upon them.

Look at Acts 6:3:

"Wherefore, brethren, look ye out among you seven men of honest report, full of the Holy Ghost and wisdom, whom we may appoint over this business."

This scripture has traditionally been referred to as the appointment of the first deacons. Notice, the "realness" of that office was already evident in their lives. These men were already living and ministering at a certain level. They were honest, which means that there must have been situations that tested their integrity. They were spirit-led, which speaks to their level of spirituality and proactiveness. They had wisdom, which means that someone must have observed how they handled challenging circumstances to the point that wisdom was displayed. These individuals were already living at a certain level. Their title just labeled them.

If you were to be labeled, what kind of title would you receive? Despite what title you have presently, if any, in all fairness how would you evaluate the real you? The real you is where you start exploring and examining your purpose and ministry. You have become several things over the years but the real you may have yet to be seen. You may have been operating in your purpose only "in part," but inside the real you is where your purpose and ministry can be clearly seen.

You must take a spiritual inventory of your core being. This is the place where your character, gifts, values and passions reside. As you reduce yourself to the least common denominator and totally yield yourself to God, you will begin to embrace the first glimpse of your ministry and purpose for life. It may not be what you currently do occupationally. It may or may not be connected to your job at the church, but it will be serving God in some dynamic capacity. You are a steward of a powerful purpose and an anointed ministry that has been personally given by God. What an awesome thought!

Because you have been given a powerful, anointed ministry, you must know that you will not move into it without a challenge from the enemy. The devil also knows that your ministry is your real purpose for living. That is the reason why he will fight you "tooth and nail" on your road to becoming what God wants you to be.

Satan sets up camp somewhere between purpose discovery and your release into actual ministry. He does not mind you knowing your purpose as long as you don't move into it. In fact, if you discover your purpose and don't act upon it, this will soon turn into frustration. Frustrated Christians are usually counter-productive and if the enemy can keep you frustrated long enough, then frustration turns to bitterness. Have you ever seen Christians that work in the church but are bitter? It is not a pretty picture. A bitter individual hinders his or her personal ministry as well as that of others.

As we journey toward our purpose and ministry, we must be mindful of the enemy's tactics and strategies to hinder us.

"Lest Satan should get an advantage of us: for we are not ignorant of his devices." 2 Corinthians 2:11

If we are mindful of these things, we can truly embrace our purpose and make ministry happen in our lives daily.

CHAPTER THREE

GOD PLACED THE MINISTRY IN YOU

"Being confident of this very thing, that he which hath begun a good work in you will perform it until the day of Jesus Christ:" Philippians 1:6

It is simply amazing that the anointed and magnificent ministry of our Lord Jesus Christ laid dormant and quiescent inside of his person for over thirty years. We saw an inkling of his greatness in light of the heavenly commotion at the nativity of his birth and during his scholarly presentation among doctors in the temple when he was twelve years old.[1] However, this is all that we see of the prolific ministry of Jesus Christ during the early part of his

---

[1] Luke 2:41-49 Now his parents went to Jerusalem every year at the feast of the Passover. 42 And when he was twelve years old, they went up to Jerusalem after the custom of the feast. 43 And when they had fulfilled the days, as they returned, the child Jesus tarried behind in Jerusalem; and Joseph and his mother knew not of it. 44 But they, supposing him to have been in the company, went a day's journey; and they sought him among their kinsfolk and acquaintance. 45 And when they found him not, they turned back again to Jerusalem, seeking him. 46 And it came to pass, that after three days they found him in the temple, sitting in the midst of the doctors, both hearing them, and asking them questions. 47 And all that heard him were astonished at his understanding and answers. 48 And when they saw him, they were amazed: and his mother said unto him, Son, why hast thou thus dealt with us? behold, thy father and I have sought thee sorrowing. 49 And he said unto them, How is it that ye sought me? wist ye not that I must be about my Father's business?

life. We know that it was in him because of these instances but the universe had to wait for its release.

You have a ministry in you that is waiting to be released. It is there because God put it there. It was set up before the foundation of the world and it was officially installed in your spiritual DNA when you were conceived in your mother's womb. Listen to what God told Jeremiah:

"Before I formed thee in the belly I knew thee; and before thou camest forth out of the womb I sanctified thee, and I ordained thee a prophet unto the nations." Jeremiah 1:5

Notice the three things that God tells Jeremiah concerning his life and predetermined ministry. "I knew you, I sanctified you," and "I ordained you." When God tells Jeremiah "I knew you" it speaks to how he already knows the totality of what his life would entail. When he says "I sanctified thee," I believe that he is letting Jeremiah know that he has set aside his life for a specific purpose. You have been set aside for a specific purpose! That's the reason why God would not let you do what others did and get away with it. That is the reason why you could not fit in every club and clique and why you may have seemed to be an outcast. It was God just sanctifying you for the ministry.

When God tells Jeremiah that he has "ordained" him as a "prophet to the nations" this is, of course, speaking of his specific ministry that was laid in Jeremiah's spirit. To ordain means to officially sanction and establish. God lets Jeremiah know, emphatically, that he has already established and officially sanctioned the ministry that is in the inner recesses of his being.

The dialogue that God has with Jeremiah also gives us a greater understanding of the essence of ministry. It appears that ministry is an entity that must be revealed because it is spiritual in nature. Its disclosure must come from its progenitor, which is God, because we cannot discern its existence naturally. God had to make known to Jeremiah what his ministry was. We know that this was "news" to Jeremiah because of his response.

"Then said I, Ah, Lord God! behold, I cannot speak: for I am a child." Jeremiah 1:6

With all of his natural senses, he still could not detect his ministry because it was in his spirit. Ministry is spiritual! Our natural senses connect us to this world in which we live. The only reason that we know about our atmospheric surroundings is because of our senses; sight, hearing, touch, taste and smell. These senses let us know that natural things exist. However, since ministry is spiritual and cannot be detected through sensory perception, its revelation must come from God. When ministry is concealed in the depths of our spirit, it remains independent of our carnal reality. However, when ministry is released, it flows thorough natural means to accomplish its work—yet still remains spiritual.

Upon further examination of this account in Jeremiah, it seems fair to suggest that each ministry has a specific task.

God told Jeremiah that he would be a "prophet to the nations." Ministry is not some fuzzy, ambiguous, religious service that is made up along the way. Ministry, God working through you, has specific objectives. For example, David was anointed to be king as a young man. He was not ready to be King, for he was a child, but Samuel's anointing was God signifying that David had a kingly ministry inside of him. Gradually, through the years, his natural side caught up to his spiritual ministry. It is imperative that we allow God to prepare us for what he has placed in us. In Colossians 4:17, Paul gives the following instructions:

"...Take heed to the ministry which thou hast received in the Lord, that thou fulfil it."

There is a specific work with several facets that God wants to bring to pass through us. We must yield ourselves to God and do all that we can to see our ministry through. God gives the promotion, but we are responsible, in part, for getting into a posture for the promotion.

"I beseech you therefore, brethren, by the mercies of God, that ye present your bodies a living sacrifice, holy, acceptable unto God, which is your reasonable service. And be not conformed to this world: but be ye transformed by the renewing of your mind, that ye may prove what is that good, and acceptable, and perfect, will of God." Romans 12:1-2

I am convinced that many individuals never experience the fullness of their ministry because they do not do their part to position themselves for it. It is not that the ministry is not there, but there is a certain disposition that God will wait for before promotion.

"For promotion cometh neither from the east, nor from the west, nor from the south. But God is the judge: he putteth down one, and setteth up another." Psalm 75:6-7

The fact of the matter is that God has placed a ministry down in your spirit. The only way to know more about it is if you yield yourself in his presence and allow him to reveal it to you. Remember, God put the ministry there for a specific reason. It is you that he wants to use to accomplish the tasks. Know that your assignment is from God and that he never makes a mistake. Thank God for the ministry in you!

"And I thank Christ Jesus our Lord, who hath enabled me, for that he counted me faithful, putting me into the ministry;" 1 Timothy 1:12

CHAPTER FOUR

THE TRANSITION INTO MINISTRY

"Therefore, seeing we have this ministry, as we have received mercy, we faint not; But have renounced the hidden things of dishonesty, not walking in craftiness, nor handling the word of God deceitfully; but by manifestation of the truth commending ourselves to every man's conscience in the sight of God."
2 Corinthians 4:1-2

Everything we do is not ministry. The majority of the things that we have done have not been ministry. Many of the things that we do, that we think are ministry, are not. This is because ministry can only happen when God's will is embraced and God's power is flowing through us. It is when God shows up in us. I have been in Christiandom for over twenty-five years and I declare to you that every activity that I have been involved with under the "Christian banner" has not had the presence of the Lord. Many of the events were positive and wholesome but God was not there as far as ministry is concerned. We know that God is omnipresent, but that is not what I am talking about.

I'm talking about the inescapable and undeniable entitlement of God, present in individuals with a ministry level of intensity that pleases the Father. I'm talking about God's anointing and approval operating by the power of the Holy Spirit!

Ministry is not manually operated. A person cannot just make up their mind to perform ministry. For ministry to transpire, an individual must come into agreement and alignment with God's divine purpose and plan. There is no ministry without God no matter how good the intentions. We don't have the authority to execute ministry nor the ability to bring it to pass. 1 Peter 4:11 states:

> "...if any man minister, let him do it as of the ability which God giveth: that God in all things may be glorified through Jesus Christ, to whom be praise and dominion for ever and ever. Amen."

It is apparent that we can carry out decent, moral and respectable works, just as long as we know that it may not fall under the category of ministry.

A few years ago, I changed my prayer concerning ministry. I used to pray, "Lord, please bless what I am doing," believing that God would come by and anoint my labor. Then it was revealed to me (I believe through something I read) that I may not be doing just what God wanted. So I changed my prayer to, "Lord, let me be a part of what you are blessing." This prayer changed our church and its many ministries, not to mention its pastor. This change in perspective and adjustment in attitude represented a shift in our spiritual paradigm and placed our ministry in the flow of God. This prayer is all about humility. It says, "Heavenly Father, sanction me to be in your will so that I can be used by you. Allow me, Lord, to cooperate within the framework of your awesome purpose and plan so that I may be center stage of your perpetual ministry." With this kind of humility you are destined to be blessed.

"Humble yourselves therefore under the mighty hand of God, that he may exalt you in due time:" 1 Peter 5:6

Humility says, "God I want to do your will and take part in your ministry."

Along with a humble disposition, it is also fair to assume that ministry must be spiritually processed through an individual. I believe that God would like to use everyone in ministry but he just can't. This is because for many, his ministry cannot be processed through them. Ministry is "stair-stepped" through your spirit into your natural man. Most have so many hindrances that ministry never makes it through. In 2 Corinthians 4:2, Paul writes concerning the ministry that we have obtained. He then proceeds to instruct us in avoiding the hindrances to ministry:

"...renounced the hidden things of dishonesty, not walking in craftiness, nor handling the word of God deceitfully;"

These are just a few things that "dam up" the flow of God. Other things may be pride, stubbornness, lack of prayer, lust, greed, jealousy, insecurities, fear, depression, complaining, anxiousness, frustration, bitterness, unforgiveness and of course, a lack of faith. This, by no means, is an exhaustive list, but the point is that the ministry that is already in you cannot come out because you have not obtained the necessary deliverance needed to be in a posture where God can use you. It's not that you are not called. It is just that you are not ready.

> *"If so be that ye have heard him, and have been taught by him, as the truth is in Jesus: That ye put off concerning the former conversation the old man, which is corrupt according to the deceitful lusts; And be renewed in the spirit of your mind; And that ye put on the new man, which after God is created in righteousness and true holiness."* Ephesians 4:21-24

Through humility and successful spiritual processing, I am convinced that ministry can flow through the people of God. This concept represents our transition into ministry. I believe that this transition must happen every time ministry occurs. Each time that God wants to use you, automatically, your humility goes on trial and your life is examined. Just because God used you yesterday does not guarantee that he will use you today. We must be continually postured before the throne of God. It is your responsibility to present the best possible you to the ministry of Jesus Christ.

"Examine yourselves, whether ye be in the faith; prove your own selves..." 2 Corinthians 13:5

CHAPTER FIVE
MINISTRY MUST BE BIRTHED OUT

"But the God of all grace, who hath called us unto his eternal glory by Christ Jesus, after that ye have suffered a while, make you perfect, stablish, strengthen, settle you." 1 Peter 5:10

There lies within each of us a powerful potential to impact God's Kingdom through anointed service. We are God's "work in progress" which encompasses our assignment of purpose. This ministry is placed in the womb of our spirit that it might experience a time of clandestine intensification within the protective environment of obscurity. At the point that it becomes conclusively prepared and has moved through the full term of its dormant development, it becomes categorically clear that the ministry must be birthed out.

It is important to understand that the birthing process for ministry consists of a period of intense painful labor through the actual release into a viable posture for God to use. For ministry to be birthed out of you, it must go through the uncomfortable movement from the internal world of private contemplation, into the external world of public occupation. This matriculation into the visible echelons of ministry is very difficult but very necessary.

> *"Because to every purpose there is time and judgment, therefore the misery (or burden) of man is great upon him."* Ecclesiastes 8:6

THE BIRTHING OF MINISTRY

Ministry must:

1. Be conceived by God in your spirit.

2. Be formed in the womb of life's experiences.

3. Be developed by proper spiritual nourishment.

4. Come "full-term" before birthing.

5. Come through labor and stress for proper birthing.

6. Be cared for with immediate attention upon birth.

7. Be nurtured into a strong, impacting ministry for the Kingdom.

Time and judgment, along with a God-ordained period of struggle, sets the stage for ministry development and production. In other words, the somewhat frustrating need of purpose fulfillment inside of you, coupled with several well placed storms in your life, enhances the maturation process for your ministry.

Like the caterpillar that must fight through the excruciating setting of the cocoon in order to develop the strong muscular wings of a butterfly, we must also endure our agonizing atmosphere, if we are to see real ministry produced. We can "fly," but not at first without struggle.

Many individuals with whom I have spoken over the years, have wanted God to eliminate the hurt and pain of their development and to lift them out of their personal struggles. But without this process their ministries would not be anointed. It is the constant wrestling and toiling that allocates the necessary fortitude and resilience for a powerful work in God. In essence, we should look for and welcome the struggle. Consider what the Apostle Paul told young Pastor Timothy:

"For the time will come when they will not endure sound doctrine; but after their own lusts shall they heap to themselves teachers, having itching ears; And they shall turn away their ears from the truth, and shall be turned unto fables. But watch thou in all things, endure afflictions, do the work of an evangelist, make full proof of thy ministry." 2 Timothy 4:3-5

Paul is letting his student know that in spite of his tenuous, unstable environment, he must go forth. He then seems to suggest that it is this platform that will provide, not only the work of his ministry, but its opportunity for growth. Timothy is instructed to let his current atmosphere "full-proof" his ministry.

It is important to understand that Satan is aware of this process also. This is the reason why he tries so diligently to confuse humankind concerning the value of our struggle and birthing process. He is angry right now that you are receiving this information! The enemy incessantly uses the strategy of intimidation to try to abort our spiritual progress. In 1 Peter 5:8, the writer tells us:

"Be sober, be vigilant; because your adversary the devil, as a roaring lion, walketh about, seeking whom he may devour:"

Satan, the original spiritual terrorist, tries to convince us to give up our ministry through scare tactics and coercion. He is banking on the fact that we will just hand over our spiritual assignment in exchange for self protection. But, remember what Jesus said concerning our assignment:

"For whosoever will save his life shall lose it; but whosoever shall lose his life for my sake and the gospel's, the same shall save it." Mark 8:35

If you are ever mugged (and I pray that you are not) there are at least three things that you can do. You can fight, try to run or hand over your wallet. Although you must assess your situation if you encounter a mugger, it is plain to see what every mugger would like. The mugger would want you to yield in the spirit of passivity and give the least amount of resistance possible. The assailant would favor you just handing over your valuables. Satan is no different. If he can threaten and terrorize you to the degree that you hand over your ministry, he has been successful. But you cannot give in to terror because that would be operating in fear. And, "...*God hath not given us the spirit of fear; but of power, and of love and of a sound mind.*" 2 Timothy 1:7

Understand that if your ministry is to be birthed out, you will face hardship and storms from your personal life as well as challenges from the enemy.

"*For we wrestle not against flesh and blood, but against principalities, against powers, against the rulers of the darkness of this world, against spiritual wickedness in high places.*" Ephesians 6:12

But know, most assuredly, that it is this platform that will nurture you most through the birthing process and into anointed and powerful ministry.

CHAPTER SIX

YOU ARE YOUR MINISTRY

"A good man out of the good treasure of his heart bringeth forth that which is good; and an evil man out of the evil treasure of his heart bringeth forth that which is evil: for of the abundance of the heart his mouth speaketh." Luke 6:45

As you embrace the fullness of your ministry, understand that it can only come forth and be presented through your character and personality. Your personal disposition is the infrastructure that your ministry is built upon. You cannot escape the fact that you and your ministry are one.

Although ministry is a spiritual entity that is separate from our humanistic mortality, it becomes a part of the human experience because of the vessel that carries it. That is why it is so important for us to optimize our standard of living, presenting the best possible framework for ministry.

I am aware of individuals that believe that their ministries are separate from the lives that they live. They believe for example, that they can preach against adultery to a congregation of people on Sunday morning, yet have an adulterous affair and still be in the will of God. Even though they may believe it's wrong to commit adultery and desire to stop, they still support the theory that their personal failure has nothing to do with their public ministry. This is a common error in Christian circles.

I believe emphatically that if you preach one thing and do another, you are living a lie! Since ministry must come through people, then in this instance, it must come through a liar. One may be fooled into believing that God honors their lives because they can charismatically get people excited or do business deals exceptionally well. But that is not the gauge of spirituality because worldly people and organizations achieve the same results. However, it is emphatically clear throughout the Bible that God pays as much attention to a person's character as he does their gifts and abilities. Our Lord Jesus Christ states in Mark 7:20-23:

> *"...That which cometh out of the man, that defileth the man. For from within, out of the heart of men, proceed evil thoughts, adulteries, fornications, murders, Thefts, covetousness, wickedness, deceit, lasciviousness, an evil eye, blasphemy, pride, foolishness: All these evil things come from within, and defile the man."*

There are many examples throughout the Scriptures concerning God's view of character and ministry. For Daniel, Esther, Peter and Paul, their character actually augmented and amplified their ministries. For individuals such as Samson, Eli and Judas, their characters essentially hindered their influence and ultimately destroyed their ministry. So, ministry effectiveness can be, at least in part, attributed to character quality. Some commentaries seem to suggest that character is a barometer for ministry success. Jesus preached right to the character of ministry leaders of the religious establishment in his day:

> "Woe unto you, scribes and Pharisees, hypocrites! for ye are like unto whited sepulchres, which indeed appear beautiful outward, but are within full of dead men's bones, and of all uncleanness."
> Matthew 23:27

Your character must reflect what you want your ministry to become. Paul presents to Timothy a rhetorical question in 1 Timothy 3:5:

> "For if a man know not how to rule his own house, how shall he take care of the church of God?"

This question seems to indicate that a man's personal dealings should be a prerequisite as to whether or not he is considered for ministry. It recommends that the individual's character be the measure of his or her level of service in God. We understand that ministry is God manifesting himself through our gifts and talents, however, this scripture along with others, seems to advise us that the possessor of the ministry becomes the driving force of its fruition.

"Drive" is an interesting word. It speaks to orchestration and control. If you want your ministry to be successful and your purpose to be fulfilled then you must learn how to drive. Driven people get results and their ministries follow that spirit. Driving also presents a unique dichotomy concerning awareness.

If you drive your car across the state to a relative's house, there are certain things that you must be cognizant of. You must pay attention to your present surroundings (road signs, people crossing the street, other vehicles changing lanes, etc.) and at the same time, not be distracted by the peripherals of the journey. In other words, driving means you must be conscious of where you are, but also focused on where you are going.

A driven recording artist will, eventually, produce CDs and DVDs over time. The ministry comes forth because the individual is driven by nature. It may take ten years of ministry development and spiritual positioning, but as the yielded vessel trusts God, maintains consciousness of their surroundings and focuses on their destination, the ministry will surely come to pass.

In the same vein, some ministries are hindered because of bad qualities. Churches will usually take on the characteristics of their pastor. If the pastor is always late, doesn't operate in integrity and is not a giver, then the church will eventually take on the same qualities. Churches, businesses and households that have no vision are led by people that have no vision:

"Where there is no vision, the people perish:" Proverbs 29:18

Remember, you are your ministry. I have a personal principle that I call the "Juke Box" theory. It says the only thing the Juke Box can play is that which is already inside. This is also true of human beings. However, I believe that through the power of God anyone can change their personal "records." If you sincerely yield yourself to our Heavenly Father and lay out before him the details of your life, you will see tremendous change, not only in your character, but in your ministry. Powerful ministry comes from those with strong character.

Chapter Seven

Every Ministry Needs A Covering

"And every open vessel, which hath no covering bound upon it, is unclean." Numbers 19:15

The power and potency of your ministry is ardently associated with your ties to God. Therefore, it is imperative that profound spiritual support systems ordained by God, be put in place. There are many things that the Lord requires of us. I truly believe that having a "covering" is one of them. Covering represents a leader that can have supervision over you and general oversight of your ministry. Hebrews 13:17 states:

"Obey them that have the rule (leadership) over you, and submit yourselves: for they watch for your souls, as they that must give account, that they may do it with joy, and not with grief: for that is unprofitable for you."

Many try to segregate this particular scripture to the local church, but I believe God's principles are the same across the board. Everyone needs a pastor. The Lord God says in Jeremiah 3:15:

"And I will give you pastors according to mine heart, which shall feed you with knowledge and understanding."

We all need knowledge and understanding.

There are several reasons why I believe that all ministries need a covering. I will discuss three of them.

1. A Covering Provides Mentorship

Whether you are a pastor, evangelist, musician, psalmist, usher, greeter, supervisor, entry-level employee, king or president, it is important that you have a spiritual mentor in your life. When I speak of a mentor, I am not talking about someone who will "pal around" with you every day. I am talking about an individual that you respect who can give you wise counsel. It is someone who can be a father or mother to you. Listen to Paul as he fathers his spiritual sons:

"I write not these things to shame you, but as my beloved sons I warn you. For though ye have ten thousand instructors in Christ, yet have ye not many fathers: for in Christ Jesus I have begotten you through the gospel. Wherefore I beseech you, be ye followers of me." 1 Corinthians 4:14-16

A mentor is someone that cares about you, prays for you and consequently carries you in his or her heart. If you are a member of a church, your pastor or pastor's spouse will provide spiritual mentorship for you.

If you are a bishop, pastor, artist, business person or just a Christian who loves the Lord, but you don't have a church home, it is time to seek a covering. Let me mention that every person that says that they are a child of God should be a member of a local church. If you are a pastor of a non-denominational church and you do not have a covering/mentor, start looking for one.

David struggled without a mentor for years. He made many mistakes that possibly could have been avoided. At one point you see him yearning for a fatherly figure.

"I looked on my right hand, and beheld, but there was no man that would know me: refuge failed me; no man cared for my soul." Psalm 142:4

Moses and Esther, in turn, were great beneficiaries of spiritual mentorship. In Exodus, Chapter 18, Moses finds himself as a leader of thousands of people. As a "good" leader, he tries to hear and address everyone's problems. His father-in-law, Jethro, mentors Moses:

"And Moses' father in law said unto him, The thing that thou doest is not good. Thou wilt surely wear away, both thou, and

this people that is with thee...I will give thee counsel and God shall be with thee:"²

Moses was blessed by the wise counsel of Jethro. Esther, also, was mentored by her uncle Mordecai. Because of her listening spirit and being in the audience of her mentor, she became the queen of that country and saved the entire nation of Israel from destruction.

2. A Covering Provides the Blessing of Accountability

I have come to the conclusion that in order to have long-term success in a business, church or home environment, preventive measures must be in place. It is necessary for leaders to observe the "big picture" and put plans in place for possible obstacles and potential infractions that may hinder the organization down the road. One of the most powerful tools, provided through covering, is accountability.

Accountability simply affords many of the vital checks and balances, over time, which keeps a ministry from drifting into the wrong areas. Most people or organizations do not plan to do wrong, they just wander into it. Accountability helps to produce balance and integrity. Having a mentor to question our actions, motives and intentions may seem rather cumbersome and awkward initially, but it will pay off in the long run.

---

² Exodus 18:17-19 And Moses' father in law said unto him, The thing that thou doest is not good. Thou wilt surely wear away, both thou, and this people that is with thee: for this thing is too heavy for thee; thou art not able to perform it thyself alone. Hearken now unto my voice, I will give thee counsel, and God shall be with thee: Be thou for the people to God-ward, that thou mayest bring the causes unto God:

KEYS TO THE COVERING

Mentorship

Accountability

Direction & Instruction

Having an official covering in your life changes your perspective and even the way that you do many things. You are more apt to do better and operate sharper when you think someone is watching you. You become more competent in your dealings and confident in your decisions when someone is covering you. A spiritual covering is part of the Biblical prescription for success.

"...and how shall they hear without a preacher? Romans 10:14

"All scripture is given by inspiration of God, and is profitable for doctrine, for reproof, for correction, for instruction in righteousness: That the man of God may be perfect, thoroughly furnished unto all good works." 2 Timothy 3:16-17

3. A Covering Provides Direction and Instruction

Many times when we do not know what to do and we do not have anyone to talk to, we make bad decisions. As leaders and as stewards of ministry, we are prone to make decisions, but if we do not have the proper resources, we have the propensity to take action "in the dark." The Bible says in Proverbs 11:14:

"Where no counsel is, the people fall: but in the multitude of counsellors there is safety."

Directions tell you where to go and instructions tell you what to do. A covering provides a point of contact that the Holy Spirit will use to give you guidance concerning your ministry and your life. Jesus said in John 16:13:

"Howbeit when he, the Spirit of truth, is come, he will guide you into all truth..."

Sometimes the source that you need is a real living person to confirm what was given in the intangible spirit realm. At times, the "spirit of truth" will come through the individual that is designated to cover you. Having someone that you trust allows you the opportunity to weigh your perception about the instructions and directions of your ministry. As you humble yourself before God, he will confirm his Word to you.

"The fear of the Lord is the beginning of knowledge: but fools despise wisdom and instruction. My son, hear the instruction

of thy father, and forsake not the law of thy mother: For they shall be an ornament of grace unto thy head and chains about thy neck." Proverbs 1:7-9

CHAPTER EIGHT

MINISTRY:
THE PROPHECY OVER YOUR LIFE

"Who hath saved us, and called us with an holy calling, not according to our works, but according to his own purpose and grace, which was given us in Christ Jesus before the world began," 2 Timothy 1:9

There is something awesomely significant about being chosen by God Almighty to carry his amazing and magnificent ministry inside of us. The idea that we possess a piece of his work for planet Earth and mankind is simply mind-boggling! According to the scripture above, it appears that, although God maintains ownership of this ministry or calling, he uses us as divine contractors to carry out this mission. If we are to be used in this manner, then it is undeniably and unquestionably true that there is a prophecy over our lives. Every prophecy is part of a God-given mandate and every mandate has a prophecy.

When God releases his ministry, simultaneously, a prophecy is put forth because God has designated a purpose for all things. Furthermore, "God is not a man, that he should lie..."[3] Whatever God has spoken and designated, it must come to pass. So, as we are stewards of this divine assignment, let us revere and hold in the highest respect God's trust of this holy designation.

Furthermore, the Word of God seems to indicate that God himself inhabits our being in order to bring his ministry to fulfillment!

"Ye are of God, little children, and have overcome them: because greater is he that is in you, than he that is in the world." 1 John 4:4

"To whom God would make known what is the riches of the glory of this mystery among the Gentiles; which is Christ in you, the hope of glory:" Colossians 1:27

God, through the power of the Holy Spirit, steps into our spirit to execute and accomplish his spiritual mandate. What powerful imagery!

So, how are we to govern ourselves under this dynamic, ever present prophecy? In the days of old, whenever a prophecy was given, it was the responsibility of the individual to "get their house in order." Sacrifices were made, altars were built and prayer and

---

[3] Numbers 23:19 God is not a man, that he should lie; neither the son of man, that he should repent: hath he said, and shall he not do it? or hath he spoken, and shall he not make it good?

fasting began, all to prepare the hearts and minds for prophecy fulfillment. They understood that they had to be in a position so that God could use them.

Not much has changed today. We must begin to consecrate ourselves so that we can be spiritually ready to be employed by God. Greater levels of prayer, fasting and worship are all in order to live under this prophecy that God has placed over your life. 1 Peter 1:13-16 says:

> "Wherefore gird up the loins of your mind, be sober, and hope to the end for the grace that is to be brought unto you at the revelation of Jesus Christ; As obedient children, not fashioning yourselves according to the former lusts in your ignorance: But as he which hath called you is holy, so be ye holy in all manner of conversation; Because it is written, be ye holy; for I am holy."

God wants to use you, so it is imperative to posture yourself so that you will be available for God and his ministry. Understand that this gift of ministry that God has laid down in your spirit goes far beyond your human existence. Remember what Paul said in 2 Timothy 1:9:

> "...which was given us in Christ Jesus before the world began."

What that means is Jesus was holding up your prophecy until you got here. But now that you are here it is time to make "full-proof" your ministry.

"Neglect not the gift that is in thee, which was given thee by prophecy, with the laying on of the hands of the presbytery. Meditate upon these things; give thyself wholly to them; that thy profiting may appear to all. Take heed unto thyself, and unto the doctrine; continue in them: for in doing this thou shalt both save thyself, and them that hear thee." 1 Timothy 4:14-16

CHAPTER NINE

MINISTRY ABUSE

"What is my reward then? Verily that, when I preach the gospel, I may make the gospel of Christ without charge, that I abuse not my power in the gospel." 1 Corinthians 9:18

As you begin to discern and assess the abundant qualities of the ministry that resides in you, it is only responsible that I mention the potential dangers of the misuse of ministry. I call it ministry abuse.

Many individuals, over time, have slipped into an unscrupulous posture of becoming a ministry abuser. It is when a person, most of the time has started out with the Lord, and leaves their spiritual "holy ground." With little spiritual standard and character infrastructure, they exploit the talents and tools of ministry to use them for their own benefit. They take advantage of God's gifts as well as his grace.

1 Timothy 4:1-2 notes:

"Now the Spirit speaketh expressly, that in the latter times some shall depart from the faith, giving heed to seducing spirits, and doctrines of devils; Speaking lies in hypocrisy; having their conscience seared with a hot iron;"

This unrighteous and immoral behavior is carefully camouflaged by the abuser so much so that the ministry appears authentic and sincere to the outside observer. It is fair to note that this activity is not ministry at all but because of the manipulation of gifts, there is a "look and feel" of genuine ministry.

These deceitful deeds are much like those of a child molester. An individual ill-uses a precious entity of ministry for selfish personal gain. The abuser seeks self-fulfillment—caring nothing about who is hurt in the process. The ministry is spiritually raped for self-indulgence and then prostituted for material gain. Those people who fit into this category have elaborate schemes to make money, secure illicit relationships and fulfill every possible fleshly desire. Listen to Paul's qualification for a bishop in Titus 1:7:

"For a bishop must be blameless, as the steward of God; not self-willed, not soon angry, not given to wine, no striker, not given to filthy lucre;"

This scripture clearly notes that we must keep God's standards to perform ministry. It is important for you not to allow yourself to slip into an unprincipled mode of operation. Some individuals willfully embrace this course of deceit, but most just drift into it. It is imperative for you to guard your anointing. If you take care of God and his ministry, he will always take care of you. This is something that the ministry abuser thinks is the way to fame and glory. However, my Bible tells me that the end of it all of it will be destruction.

"There is a way that seemeth right unto a man, but the end thereof are the ways of death." Proverbs 16:25

Jesus declared in John 14:6:

"...I am the way, the truth, and the life: no man cometh unto the Father, but by me."

If you ever find yourself in an amoral posture or are currently experiencing it right now, understand that you must take action immediately! You will have to fight your flesh and the associated demons that have attached themselves to your situation. There is hope, however, through the ministry of Jesus Christ. In fact, Paul talks about this very thing in 2 Corinthians 5:17-21:

"Therefore if any man be in Christ, he is a new creature: old things are passed away; behold, all things become new. And all things are of God, who hath reconciled us to himself by Jesus Christ, and hath given to us the ministry of reconciliation; To wit, that God was in Christ, reconciling the world unto himself, not imputing their trespasses unto them; and hath committed unto us the word of reconciliation. Now then we are ambassadors

for Christ, as though God did beseech you by us: we pray you in Christ's stead, be ye reconciled to God. For he hath made him to be sin for us, who knew no sin; that we might be made the righteousness of God in him."

I believe that God will restore anyone that seeks restoration. Trust him and turn your life around. Embrace him once again and get ready for real ministry.

CHAPTER TEN

REAL MINISTRY SUCCESS HAS SUCCESSION

"Having therefore obtained help of God, I continue unto this day, witnessing both to small and great, saying none other things than those which the prophets and Moses did say should come: That Christ should suffer, and that he should be the first that should rise from the dead, and should shew light unto the people, and to the Gentiles." Acts 26:22-23

It is important for you to realize that the ministry that is in your "legal custody" does not belong to you. You are the official steward, guardian and caretaker, but its ownership remains with the Heavenly Father. Understand that this most prolific and spiritually operative entity is designed with you in mind, however, its heavenly mission is connected to a plan that goes far beyond your human existence.

No matter how special your ministry may seem, nor how great the results it may yield, your ministry is profoundly engaged in what I call "the Big Plan." I know my wife thinks I am crazy sometimes because while in the midst of going through a crisis or experiencing some wonderful highs associated with ministry, I will lean over to her and say, "This is part of the Big Plan."

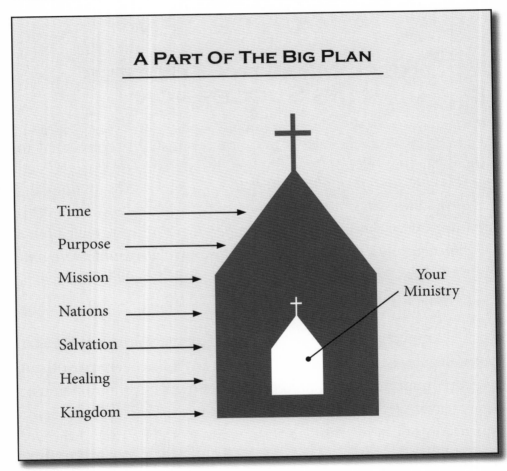

A PART OF THE BIG PLAN

Time

Purpose

Mission

Nations

Salvation

Healing

Kingdom

Your Ministry

Ministry is much more than how many people we fed at the homeless shelter, how many people we counseled last year, how many members we have or the size of our buildings. Ministry is about accomplishing the unmitigated will of God during this dispensational time period. Don't get me wrong, these things are wonderful and help the Kingdom of God, but he has an overall strategic plan that will heal, deliver and save nations when it is through. We must be cognizant that our personal ministry along with the ministry at our local church, is a part of this comprehensive and extensive program. We must not become "tunnel visioned" into thinking that our ministry is our particularized island that is disconnected from other ministries of the Kingdom.

The fact of the matter is that your ministry is connected to something that has been around long before you got here and will be here long after you're gone. The writer in Jude verse 3 states:

"Beloved, when I gave all diligence to write unto you of the common salvation, it was needful for me to write unto you, and exhort you that ye should earnestly contend for the faith which was once delivered unto the saints."

Notice that it was only once delivered. The Christian movement was issued by God Almighty only once; but it has been carried out by the ministry that has been placed within us from generation to generation.

So, the ministry that you possess along with its corresponding gifts, talents and abilities are not only God's, but are linked to a greater cause than what we see. Success in ministry deals with you being able to work your "shift" to accomplish the mission designated in the overall plan of God. With this in mind, we can view our part in ministry from a different perspective. Our goals should be to do the best that we can from the time we take the handoff from the last generation until the time we release the baton to the next.

The genuine merit of ministry success is succession. Real power is in the efficacy of ministry over time. One should question ministries that crop up overnight and are gone tomorrow. We should pay close attention to organizations and individuals that operate on their own or are only around for a limited time. We should even take inventory concerning what our ministry is about. Will it succeed when we are gone? Is it connected to God's overall plan?

Consider this: if your ministry dies when you die it may have been just your ministry and not God's. We must be careful to ensure that the ministries that we build, are not built around us, but built around God.

"Feed the flock of God which is among you, taking the oversight thereof, not by constraint, but willingly; not for filthy lucre, but of a ready mind; Neither as being lords over God's heritage, but being ensamples to the flock. And when the chief Shepherd shall appear, ye shall receive a crown of glory that fadeth not away." 1 Peter 5:2-4

THE SEASONS OF MINISTRY

As necessary as it is to understand the mechanics of the "Big Plan," it is equally important to understand the seasons within the "Big Plan" concerning your ministry. Success and succession are dependent upon how we handle the given phases of our ministry development.

It is essential that we comprehend that what our ministry looks like today may not be what it will look like tomorrow. This is because, although it is the same ministry and we are the same people, the season will dictate what is brought out where mission is concerned. I was an Army Officer and as I look back to my years in the service, my role changed, even though I never left the service.

Take the seasons of motherhood for example. A young mother has a responsibility to care for her children while learning and struggling through the challenging environment of maternal functionality and womanhood. A seasoned mother has her trials of multi-tasking with domestic responsibility and, through it all, is better equipped to handle adolescent and young adult children. A grandmother, on the other hand, has a significantly different role of providing wisdom and support. All three function in motherhood, but they are in significantly different seasons.

Ministry is similar. Knowledge, temperament, attitude, experience, surroundings, timing and atmosphere all have to do with what level of ministry is displayed and what will ultimately define the season. My ministry is a whole lot different today than it was ten years ago. I expect it to be unquestionably different ten years from now. It is still the same ministry, but in a different season.

To be effective, it is key that we discern the seasonal time of each stage of our ministry. We cannot reach succession if we are not first successful.

"To everything there is a season, and a time to every purpose under the heaven:" Ecclesiastes 3:1

I have come to the conclusion that many of us misinterpret our season, therefore rendering ourselves ineffective. We are sedentary and inactive at the time we should be moving, or we are mobilizing during the period that God wants us still. This misinterpretation brings about activity that is unsuccessful and unproductive.

On the farm, if you pick the fruit too soon, the fruit is wasted. If you wait too late in the season, then the fruit is rotten. Productivity has all to do with laboring in the right season. Some individuals are moving ahead of God. It is not that they are not called, but they need to be trained.

"…let us wait on our ministering; or he that teacheth, on teaching; Or he that exhorteth, on exhortation: he that giveth, let him do it with simplicity; he that ruleth, with diligence; he that sheweth mercy, with cheerfulness." Romans 12:7-8

These individuals have "zeal not according to knowledge"[4] and essentially end up making a mess of their ministries. They are "half-baked" ministers. They have all the right ingredients but they did not stay in the oven long enough.

On the other hand, there are those who should be further along. The writer in Hebrews says:

"For when for the time ye ought to be teachers, ye have need that one teach you again which be the first principles of the oracles of God; and are become such as have need of milk, and not of strong meat. For every one that useth milk is unskilful in the word of righteousness: for he is a babe." Hebrews 5:12-13

What a tragedy it is to be willfully stuck in old things when God has called you to higher levels. Respond to God's calling in the proper season.

There are also times when God will retire at least a part of the ministry from you and graduate it through "successional handoff" to someone else. Many times people have a hard time releasing something that has been a part of them for several years. Others may have difficulty accepting God's process, but we must be mindful that this ministry belongs to God and not us. If he designates someone else to take that task, let it go. If you don't release it, the ministry succession may be hindered and

---

[4] Romans 10:2 For I bear them record that they have a zeal of God, but not according to knowledge.

hanging on to what God told you to let go of may become a bigger problem.

Be assured that God always knows what he is doing. Since God is in control, your new set of responsibilities will be positive and your ministry will always match your new season.

CHAPTER ELEVEN
MINISTRY CHECK UP

"For I will restore health unto thee, and I will heal thee of thy wounds, saith the Lord; because they called thee an Outcast, saying, This is Zion, whom no man seeketh after." Jeremiah 30:17

I had been a pastor for a couple of years and things did not seem to be going too well. We were renting space at a local high school with very little money and no additional resources coming in, we were very limited. We were maintaining, but wondering "is this all that God is going to do concerning our ministry?" I was a frustrated preacher. Before long I had slipped into a mode of complaining and there was a feeling of irritation every time church service rolled around: "God is this what you called me to do?"

It was around this time I entered into earnest fervent prayer and counseling with my wife and mentors. I was directed to work on me—to change my personal disposition. After following these directives, I started feeling better. I laid many of my personal issues and burdens on the altar and worked diligently to improve my personal relationships, including my marriage (which I had neglected since starting the church). Personal things started to look up.

As I began to regain focus on the church, I noticed something. The church had gotten better! Attendance had increased, offerings were up and excitement was renewed. I continued on the same course. It was then I began to see the trend. Whenever I got better, the church got better. The Apostle Paul appears to demonstrate this principle as he sent Pastor Timothy, a man of character, to be the leader of a church:

"For this cause have I sent unto you Timotheus, who is my beloved son, and faithful in the Lord, who shall bring you into remembrance of my ways which be in Christ, as I teach every where in every church." 1 Corinthians 4:17

Ministry is healthy when the vessel that carries it is healthy. You must develop the total man physically, mentally and spiritually. It is important for you to eat right and exercise. I have found that when I eat healthy foods and have a disciplined program of consistent exercise, I tend to feel better, think sharper and have more energy for ministry and my family.

It is a good thing to keep improving yourself mentally. This means being well read along with regular Bible study. Reading books that are wholesome will build you up mentally as well as spiritually. There should also be a selection of readings that challenge you to go to the next level in your walk with God. This will have a profound effect on your ministry. Also, it is a good idea to pursue a degree in your field of study or obtain a certification in some relevant discipline. This will only enhance your ministry.

As we have mentioned throughout the book, continue to consecrate yourself before the Lord. Fasting, praying and personal devotional times alone with God, together with regular church attendance at worship services and Bible Teaching is important. Special seminars and conferences can also be an enhancement to your ministry. You need to be in a yielded spiritual posture in order to be powerfully used for your ministry.

"Beloved, I wish above all things that thou mayest prosper and be in health, even as thy soul prospereth." 3 John, verse 2

CHAPTER TWELVE

MINISTRY AND THE GLEANERS' BLESSING

"And he gave some, apostles; and some, prophets; and some, evangelists; and some, pastors and teachers; For the perfecting of the saints, for the work of the ministry, for the edifying of the body of Christ:" Ephesians 4:11-12

In Bible days, there was a wonderful custom called gleaning. Gleaning was a practice implemented during the time of harvest when the laborers would bring in the fruitful yield of the season. The gleaning directive would instruct the workers to leave a portion of the harvest in the field so that the poor and travelers could take advantage of the crop. Most of the time, the recipients would not eat the field produce but would take it to the market to sell. This would give them much needed income for their families and travels. This was a wonderful way of helping to balance out the economic structure of their community.

God's ministry has a gleaning quality to it. You cannot participate in God's ministry without it leaving a blessing in your life. As we work for God, this potent ministry that he has given us makes a tremendous impact on the Kingdom of God. The anointing that comes with this ministry is left on the life of the believer. So, not only is the Kingdom blessed, the vessel that carries the ministry is also blessed because it receives the residual anointing.

> "And it shall come to pass in that day, that his burden shall be taken away from off thy shoulder, and his yoke from off thy neck, and the yoke shall be destroyed because of the anointing." Isaiah 10:27

One day I was reading the scripture concerning the work of the ministry when it occurred to me that there is an awesome benefit to being used by God in ministry. You cannot cover God's Kingdom with your ministry gift and not affect your own circumstance! If I have power in God's Kingdom, it starts with my personal life and in my house. As ministry works it way out of you, it conquers every ungodly thing it passes. If you are positioned right, great things will come to pass. Jesus said in Mark 16:17-18:

> "And these signs shall follow them that believe; In my name shall they cast out devils; they shall speak with new tongues; They shall take up serpents; and if they drink any deadly thing, it shall not hurt them; they shall lay hands on the sick, and they shall recover."

This is the gleaners' reward of ministry. Taking on the work of ministry qualifies the believer for the full benefit package—medical, household and even life. How about coverage for your children? Now, how much would you pay?

"For the promise is unto you, and to your children, and to all that are afar off, even as many as the Lord our God shall call." Acts 2:39

Lyle and Deborah Dukes Ministries
P.O. Box 431
Woodbridge, VA 22194
(703) 490-4040
8-PSTOR-DUKES / (877) 867-3853 (toll free)
mail@harvestlifechangers.com
www.harvestlifechangers.com

Harvest Life Changers World Ministries
P.O. Box 4514
Woodbridge, VA 22194
(703) 490-4040
8-PSTOR-DUKES / (877) 867-3853 (toll free)
mail@harvestlifechangers.com
www.harvestlifechangers.com

About Pastor Lyle Dukes & Co-Pastor Deborah Dukes and Harvest Life Changers Church, International

Pastor and Co-Pastor Dukes have been commissioned by God to reach the world and change lives through the preaching and teaching of God's Word. It is their desire to see every believer broken free from the chains of bondage and walking progressively in the manifestation of God's promises.

Over the past ten years, Harvest has become a life-changing place of growth and deliverance through the power of Jesus Christ. God has continued to send souls to hear these anointed and appointed vessels. Today, the church has over 4,000 members and countless visitors who come to worship God, be saved, delivered and set free.

If you are ever in the Woodbridge, Virginia area, we invite you to worship with us on Sundays at 8:00 am, 9:00 am and 11:30 am and on Wednesdays for Pastoral Bible Teaching at 7:30 pm.

For additional information, you may call (877) 867-3853 or visit www.harvestlifechangers.com.

Want A Richer, More Fulfilling Prayer Life That Gets Results?

Let Us Pray will kindle in your spirit a passion for frequent and fervent prayer that will change your life forever!

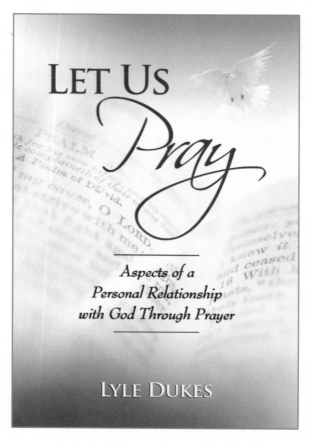

Order this powerful book by phone or online!
8-PSTOR-DUKES / (877) 867-3853
www.harvestlifechangers.com

To request a Lyle and Deborah Dukes Ministries Product Catalog call us toll free or write to Lyle and Deborah Dukes Ministries, P.O. Box 431, Woodbridge, Virginia 22194

Are You Receiving All Of Your Benefits?

Lyle and Deborah Dukes will teach you the steps to actively pursue God's will in any and every situation, ensuring that you come out with the best possible results!

Order this powerful book by phone or online!
8-PSTOR-DUKES / (877) 867-3853
www.harvestlifechangers.com

To request a Lyle and Deborah Dukes Ministries Product Catalog call us toll free or write to Lyle and Deborah Dukes Ministries, P.O. Box 431, Woodbridge, Virginia 22194

Do You Know Nothing Can Stop You From Reaching Your Destiny?

Don't settle for anything less than what God has for you. Take hold of the teaching in this life-changing book and begin to experience a life of victory through Jesus Christ!

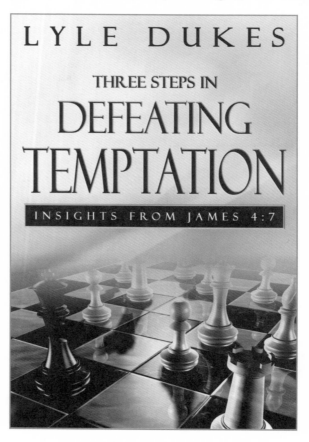

Order this powerful book by phone or online!
8-PSTOR-DUKES / (877) 867-3853
www.harvestlifechangers.com

To request a Lyle and Deborah Dukes Ministries Product Catalog call us toll free or write to Lyle and Deborah Dukes Ministries, P.O. Box 431, Woodbridge, Virginia 22194

Do You Want To Live Victoriously?

Let Lyle Dukes give you the yoke-destroying, bondage-breaking truth that will propel you into your destiny!

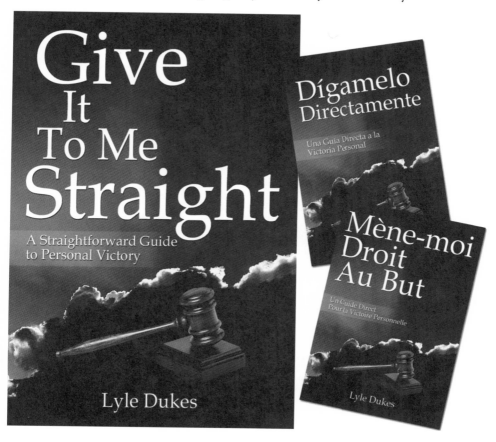

Harvest Life Changers Church, International Mass Choir

Order this Top 20 CD by phone or online!
8-PSTOR-DUKES / (877) 867-3853
www.harvestlifechangers.com

To request a Lyle and Deborah Dukes Ministries Product Catalog call us toll free or write to Lyle and Deborah Dukes Ministries, P.O. Box 431, Woodbridge, Virginia 22194

Harvest Life Changers Church, International Mass Choir

He's Right There

Order this soul-stirring CD by phone or online!
8-PSTOR-DUKES / (877) 867-3853
www.harvestlifechangers.com

To request a Lyle and Deborah Dukes Ministries Product Catalog call us
toll free or write to Lyle and Deborah Dukes Ministries, P.O. Box 431,
Woodbridge, Virginia 22194

COME VISIT THE HARVEST!

HARVEST LIFE CHANGERS CHURCH, INTERNATIONAL

14401 TELEGRAPH ROAD · WOODBRIDGE, VIRGINIA 22192

(703) 490-4040 · www.harvestlifechangers.com

If you are ever in the Woodbridge, Virginia area, we invite you to worship with us during our Sunday services and on Wednesdays for Pastoral Bible Teaching!

SERVICE SCHEDULE

Sunday Services

8:00 am......9:00 am......11:30 am

Youth Church is available during the 11:30 am service (Pre-K3 - Grade 5)

Wednesday

Prayer.................................7:00 pm
Pastoral Bible Teaching....7:30 pm
Youth Ministry...................7:30 pm

Directions: From I-95, take exit 158B (Prince William Pkwy) toward Manassas. Turn left onto Telegraph Road. Follow the road three quarters of a mile and look for the Potomac Mills highway sign on the left. Harvest Life Changers Church is located at 14401 Telegraph Road, behind IKEA.

All are welcome!

PASTOR LYLE DUKES & CO-PASTOR DEBORAH DUKES

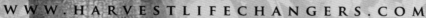